The Beginner's Guide to Indoor and Miniature Gardening

Understanding Indoor Gardens, Miniature Gardens, and Gardens in a Bottle

Healthy Gardening Series

Dueep Jyot Singh

Mendon Cottage Books

JD-Biz Publishing

Download Free Books!

http://MendonCottageBooks.com

All Rights Reserved.

No part of this publication may be reproduced in any form or by any means, including scanning, photocopying, or otherwise without prior written permission from JD-Biz Corp Copyright © 2015

All Images Licensed by Fotolia and 123RF.

Disclaimer

The information is this book is provided for informational purposes only. It is not intended to be used and medical advice or a substitute for proper medical treatment by a qualified health care provider. The information is believed to be accurate as presented based on research by the author.

The contents have not been evaluated by the U.S. Food and Drug Administration or any other Government or Health Organization and the contents in this book are not to be used to treat cure or prevent disease.

The author or publisher is not responsible for the use or safety of any diet, procedure or treatment mentioned in this book. The author or publisher is not responsible for errors or omissions that may exist.

Warning

The Book is for informational purposes only and before taking on any diet, treatment or medical procedure, it is recommended to consult with your primary health care provider.

Check out some of the other Health Learning Series books at Amazon.com

[Gardening Series on Amazon](#)

[Health Learning Series on Amazon](#)

Download Free Books!

http://MendonCottageBooks.com

Table of Contents

Introduction 4
Necessary Tools for Bottle Gardening 8
Best Plants for Bottle Gardening 11
Small Plant Gardens 21
Indoor Small Plant Garden Combinations 23
Pot et Fleur 26
Making a Moss Garden 27
Knowing More about Moss 29
Growing Plants from Pips 31
Exotic gardening – Pineapple Tops 33
Miniature Gardens 34
Trees 37
Miniature Roses 39
Other Popular Tiny Plants 39
Taking Care of Your Miniature Garden 41
Bulbs for Your Garden 42
    Selecting the Right Bulbs 42

    Planting Your Bulbs 43

Planting Hyacinth and Crocus Corms 45
Bulb Fiber – Tips 47
Newspaper Compost 48
"Plunging" Bulbs 50
Growing Bulbs on Water 52
Methods of Water Cultivation 52
Bulb Failure 53
Best Bulbs Choices 53
Conclusion 55
Author Bio 56
Publisher 66

Introduction

The first time I saw a miniature garden growing in a bottle, my immediate response was "but how did the plants get into the bottle?" Naturally, this amused the gardener very much, and for those people who are not into the secret of how the plants got into the bottle, this feat can only be on par with how did a model ship get into the bottle!

A garden in a bottle has about the same sort of fascination and requires almost that same amount offered dexterity and ingenuity to construct as a ship in the bottle. It is also going to need a lot of patience, because after all, you are gardening in limited space. But once your water garden is established, it can be left for months without attention. In many cases, depending on your plans, it may also not need watering.

So for all those people who have been really fascinated with this conversation piece, when you see people surrounding a glass bottle with beautiful plants growing in it, here is the beginner's guide to indoor gardening in a bottle.

More than 200 years ago, a London physician named that Nathaniel Ward discovered that mosses, as well as ferns, which never grew satisfactorily in a city full of industrial fumes flourished if they were grown in the protection of a glass sided case. Thanks to his experiments, bottle Gardens developed in Europe, and since then, they have been the rage all over the world for people who are strapped for place, are looking for a new hobby, and also want to achieve something wonderful.

You can use any large bottle. But the bottle has to be made of glass! Carboy glass bottles are normally made for brewing beer, so if you can get them cheap at a nursery nearby, please do so.

A 5 gallon carboy bottle is going for around USD48 on eBay USA, but as my gardening books always suggest, follow and advocate minimum of expense and minimum of fuss, you may want to spend some time asking around in your circle of friends and neighbors for large glass bottles, which is they can spare you.

I have seen some of these bottles kept away in garages, because once upon a time, they were used and the owner does not have any use for them at the moment. He may not want them for another 20 years, either. Please do buy the bottles from your friends!

Otherwise, a long-lasting friendship can get into jeopardy, when carelessly spoken words of half jesting "Well, he borrowed that bottle from me and what a mess he has made in it." could cause subconscious rancor and ill will. That is of course if he is not interested in gardening!

If he is a gardener, he is going to demand his bottle back – along with your bottle garden, - five years down the line!

You may want to tell him the purpose for this gardening experiment. It is possible he may also want to give you some suggestions about plants based on his experience.

Wash and dry the bottle. With the means of the funnel introduce 2 inches of gravel which is going to be used for draining, and then several inches of dry compost into your bottle. I prefer natural organic compost with limestone, sand, and even potting compost is going to do very well. You can also add a little bit of dry soil mixed with crushed charcoal.

This carboy glass bottle is used for brewing beer. But instead, we can use the funnel for placing soil at the bottom of the bottle.

Make sure that the soil is dry. Damp soil is not going to go very easily down the funnel. Also, damp soil clings to the side of the bottle.

Now, as bottle Gardens are Gardens in miniature, you have to introduce only small plants into them.

Necessary Tools for Bottle Gardening

Here are the implements which you will need for successful bottle gardening, including lots of patience and enthusiasm. Make sure that the mouth of the bottle is wide enough to allow the introduction of a fork and a dessert spoon.

A small desert spoon is going to be your shovel!

In the same manner you are going to be using the fork to dig up the soil. Lash the fork and the spoon with tape or with wire to thin bamboo canes.

They are going to pass easily through the neck of the bottle. They can then be manipulated carefully to cover to the roots of the plants with soil.

Even if this is not done very efficiently in the beginning, the plants will after watering soon root afresh in the humidity of the glass container.

You can also use a paper funnel to insert the dry soil into the bottle. A paper funnel has a wider mouth than an ordinary funnel.

After you have planted them, the water is introduced by means of a small can or with a narrow mouthed tube. Now add another half an inch layer of gravel on top of the compost, so that your plants can be seen, and also so that this gravel and compost acts as mulch, especially in cold weather

Once the planting has been finished cork the bottle tightly. When my gardener friend told me this, my first reaction was, hey, do not the plants need air? But he told me that the idea was to establish a completely closed atmosphere, which is self-watering.

This was a miniature and natural rainforest, where the water passed off from the leaves condensed on the glass sides of the bottle and returned back to the roots. It seems the large size of the container has enough air trapped in it, for the small plants to grow and flourish. This is the reason why a bottle garden needs watering very rarely. He watered his bottle garden once a year!

Stand the bottle in a good light, but not strong sunlight. If the core is fitted with a lamp holder, a bottle garden makes an excellent floor lamp or a table lamp in which the subtle beauties of a growing garden can grace your room night and day.

Someone just asked me whether they could leave the bottle uncorked. Well, why not, if you remember to water them every three weeks. Uncorked bottles means that they are getting plenty of fresh air, and the soil is drying out. So if you are leaving your bottles uncorked, that means watering about once a month. Be careful while watering. Overwatering means swamping them. And because your bottle does not have a drainage hole, they are going to suffer from roof rot.

Do not overcrowd your plants. Four – Five plants are quite enough for one large bottle.

Best Plants for Bottle Gardening

You may just start your experiment by growing ordinary seeds.

The best plants for bottle gardening are of course those which like moist and close atmospheres and conditions.

Just imagine small plants which love a moist humid atmosphere, and were basically native to rainforests.

If you are corking your bottle, you can use these plants.

Aglaonema commutatum – dark green leaves with silver gray spots

Begonia foliosa – fuschia Begonia – this is a shrubby plant with glossy and small green leaves.

Zebrina pendula – Wandering Jew – silvery gray and green leaves with dark green margins and purple stripes down the center

Billbergia nutans – Queens Tears – green and gray leaves with very showy, thick bracts and green and purple flowers

Dracaena godseffiana – gold dust Dracaena – dark green leaves thickly spotted with cream.

Pilea muscosa – blue-green minute leaves, Pilea varieties have attractive leaves. One of these plants is called Creeping Charlie

Cryptanthus bivittatus roseo pictus – pink leaves with green stripes. Put them in the shade and they are going to turn dark green or light green.

Saintpaulia ionantha- the varieties of this particular plant has flowers ranging from deep purple to white and violet. **These are our favorite African violets**

Pepperomia species like *mommularifolia* , – round stalked leaves with threadlike and creeping stems –, *obtusifolia* – fleshy and dark green leaves with a purple edge – and *magnoliaefolia* – mid-green leaves with cream irregular margin.

Dracaena sanderi- grayish green leaves with ivory cream margins.

Also Ferns like:

Pteris cretica – pale Brown or straw colored fronds.

Asplenium nidus – dark green straw shaped and shiny fern.

Davallia bullata – broad, dark green plant with leathery leaves. This is also known as a deerfoot fern.

Adiantum capillus veneris- commonly known as the maidenhair fern. These have delicate and light green fronds.

You can get smaller varieties of these ferns which is anywhere in your nearest nursery.

You may also want to ask your friendly neighborhood professional nursery man or gardener, to tell you all about small plants which grow well in your locality.

Small Plant Gardens

We have learned more about bottle gardens, but what about houseplants, which are not in themselves particularly showy and striking. Try mixing them in plant gardens in dishes or in large bowls. Many houseplants do better in a community.

I had this huge shallow earthenware clay pot, in which I used to make yogurt. Being a clay pot, one day it cracked. And as I could not use it to make yogurt from creamy milk anymore, I decided that I was going to plant a mixed indoor plant garden in that bowl.

Thankfully, I have a garden, a terrace, as well as bow windows, which are very sunny. So I could plant plants, which grew well in shade, and also enjoyed the sun.

Fill the bowl with your favorite potted compost. My preferred compost is one with organic manure, soil, which drains well, gravel, and sand. I also add limestone in small quantities, and a little bit of crushed charcoal. Now I arrange the plants on the surface to get some idea of the composition before turning them out of their garden beds or original pots

Indoor Small Plant Garden Combinations

Philodendrons are easy to obtain, and are sturdy plants.

You can try this Combination– *Sansevieria nahnii ,Sedum sieboldii mediovariegatum, [October Daphne] Filea cadierei nana, [aluminium plant] Zebrine quadricolor, Ficus fumila, [creeping or climbing fig] and Tolmiea menzisii [the Piggy back plant] and Philodendron scadens.*

The plants themselves are chosen for contrasting textures and shapes as well as colors.

Plant these plants formally interspersing a few small pieces of rock. If desired. Then cover the surface of the soil with chippings of granite and coarse sand.

Take great care not to overwater these plants, especially during the winter season. Small plant gardens that are kept in centrally heated rooms are going to lose moisture fast. That is why they need more water in winter, than those in colder rooms.

Creeping figs are excellent as wall climbers outdoors. They are also excellent indoor plants when grown in contained areas.

Pot et Fleur

You can also make a lovely and unusual declaration for a party or a dinner table by making your temporary plant garden for the occasion.

Dig up the plants from the outside garden. Arrange them artistically in a bowl. Push metal funnels into the soil between the plants. These metal funnels can easily be bought for this purpose. Fill the funnels up with water and stand the fresh-cut blooms in them. This combination of growing plants arranged with cut flowers is called pot et fleur.

This is a lost Victorian art. Many horticulturists and flowering arrangement trainers nowadays just stick cut flowers into a plastic pot, and call it pot et Fleur. This is not the right nomenclature nor is it the original thing.

The original art form included plants as well as flowers, growing in a pot for a special occasion. After the party was over, back the plants went to their own specially allocated places in the garden.

Making a Moss Garden

Now this is something which I find very fascinating because I spent my childhood and youth in areas where it rained continuously. That is why the walls and every available surface, including trees were always covered with a layer of soft cushioning Moss.

The best time of the year to make it Moss Garden is midwinter. This is when the mosses grow in the woods and are at their best. This is, of course, if you are living in an atmosphere full of moisture, where the rain allows mosses to grow. Sorry, as far as I know ,Moss gardens cannot be made in desert arid areas.

Dig out chumps of all kinds of mosses – the search for them makes a pleasant outing on a mild wintry morning.

Knowing More about Moss

Moss is a green plant which grows as a mossy cushion in areas full of high water content. This is flowerless and propagates itself with spores. These spores grow in stalked Brown capsules.

During the Second World War, when Britain, which was notoriously ill-prepared in supplies, as well as in training found itself without medicines, they fell back to an ancient natural healing remedy, which they had learned from the Scotch and from the Gauls – using Moss to heal.

Moss is considered to be about 50 times more absorbent than cotton! So when the wounded warriors came limping home, the good wife of the house immediately gathered a handful of moss from the nearest wall and pressed it to remove all the moisture. After that, she clamped this mossy handful over the wound, and bound it up. And then she allowed the wound to heal naturally.

So many weekends were spent by British women in collecting these Moss plans from their carpets in sacks, and then sending them to the hospitals. So after you have collected lots of moss, arranges them in a flat dish. You can use a tray. Take care that no Moss overlaps or straggles over the dish's edge or it is going to act as a siphon and dry out your garden.

The Moss should be sprayed with water once each week. More watering is necessary if you live in an atmosphere where the moisture content in the atmosphere is less. Mosses love damp atmospheres.

You can add color and variety by adding to Moss gardens, some pansy or violet roots or primrose roots between the patches of moss. You can also stick in one or two winter blossoms gathered fresh from the garden. However, the contrasts of texture and color of one Moss with another, are quite interesting enough to warrant the uses of just mosses alone in your moss garden.

Growing Plants from Pips

Charming little plants can be grown from pips or seeds discarded from your dessert plate. I normally collect the seeds from citrus fruit, dates, and even avocado. I never allow my lemon seeds or orange seeds to dry out because that means that I am never going to have a little orange tree growing in a pot. So after I have finished with the fruit, I just pop in the seeds in a cup full of water to keep them moist.

For planting plants with pips, take a 12 – 18 inch pot. You have miniature orange tree varieties, but they are, of course, best for bonsai gardening or miniature gardening. Your lemon tree flourishes best at temperatures between 55°F and 60°F – 13°C to 20°C.

Lemon trees love a little bit of sun, so after you have planted them in your pot which had been filled previously with compost, organic fertilizer, a little bit of sand and gravel, rich loamy soil, and leaf humus, just sow your seeds, cover with soil, and water. The soil should be well drained.

Avocados germinated more quickly leave the seeds are soaked in water for hours – 48 or so – then placed the large side down on a glass surface. The base of your avocado seed should just touch the water. Once the roots have formed plant your avocado in sandy soil.

Exotic gardening – Pineapple Tops

Try something new. Try growing a pineapple. Cut off the leafy top of a pineapple with a thin segment of the upper rind and leave it for a day or so to dry. Then pot it carefully in very sandy soil and put it in a warm place to root. You can stand it on a box of peat , for example, over a warm radiator. Not every pineapple top is going to "take" but if one does, put it in fairly rich soil and keep it in a warm light place. Do not overwater your new exotic pineapple plant.

I have not seen many pineapple plants grown in this way bearing fruit, but if they are placed in a warm greenhouse, you may strike lucky.

Miniature Gardens

I found miniature gardens to be a fascinating form of indoor gardening. This is where you construct and cultivate complete and tiny gardens. These miniature gardens can be made in almost any container – a flat vegetable dish, a large bowl, an old-fashioned tray, which you can pick up at a street market stall or even a baking tin.

Miniature gardens give particular pleasure in winter and early spring, when flowers are scarce and you spend more time indoors.

If your chosen container has drainage holes, so much the better. But they are not essential. Indeed, they pose the problem of protecting your polished furniture on which you are going to stand your miniature garden. That means you will need to put a tray underneath the garden container.

So regardless of whether or not your container has drainage holes, cover the base, with 1 inch layer of small stones, pieces of broken pottery, and pebbles; these are going to drain the moisture from the soil above and keep the plant roots from standing in water. Next spread a thin layer of leaves or even pieces of coarse peat to prevent the finer soil from sifting through the holes.

After that, you are going to add the soil. Choose the best potting compost, available in the nursery, but do not add fertilizer react. You can also make a mixture of coarse sand, loam, peat, brick rubble and crushed charcoal.

Your miniature garden can be designed in as many different ways as you design an ornery full-scale garden. If it is going to be a miniature of London,

while the soil evenly to give an informal effect. Introduce small pieces of natural stone here and there.

Picture - Bottle Garden Anne-Lise Heinrichs
http://www.flickr.com/photos/snigl3t/414712990/

If you are going to make a formal garden, make sunken beds and little paths around small lawns. You can use thin pieces of stone or slate for walls and pathways. This is where you are going to use your ingenuity, imagination and creativity.

The lawns are sown with grass seed. You can keep them trimmed with nail scissors. Some of the loveliest miniature gardens are made in Japanese-style with small bridges, temples, and even small ornaments. You can make sunken pools with meat paste jars.

Whichever style is chosen, the aim is to keep trees, stones, and plants all in proportion.

Trees

The trees for your miniature garden are going to include – dwarf Evergreen Piceas varieties. The trees which are going to give height to your miniature garden.

I really like a tiny conifer which belongs to the Cypress family. It is called *chamaecyparis obtusa ericoides*. This makes a dome shaped tree a few inches high and wide. While exploring and adventuring in the mountain fastnesses of Ladakh, more than two decades ago, I was fascinated with these fully grown plants growing in those arid regions and in a miniature form. What a haven for bonsai gardeners.

With all the knowledge of plant taxonomy and nomenclature fresh in my head, – I had just left University – it was "a heavenly paradise of exquisite plants, " especially some plants which I had never seen before, anywhere else while exploring. Also, there were larger varieties, which had adapted themselves to miniature shapes in the climate and yet functioned as full-grown plants.

So go to your nearest nursery and ask them whether they have dwarf tree varieties. You can also plant Beech seedlings and dwarf oak in your miniature garden. These are going to last for a few years, before they grow too big. Then you are going to take those plants out carefully and plant them in your large garden for them to flourish for hundreds of years.

There is another suitable tree for your miniature garden – dwarf juniper – *Juniperus communis compressa* . Junipers and conifers are good-looking, and also rather if one would permit the word, cute.

Most small bulbs looked well in miniature garden. You may try snowdrops, crocus, dwarf cyclamen and Narcissus. A small bulb that produces red flowers throughout most of the summer is *Rhodohypoxis baurii*. This plant grows just 4 inches high!

This attractive plant is called Emily Peel.

Miniature Roses

Dwarf variety of miniature roses are excellent for your miniature garden. *Rosa roulettii* forms of miniature roses are just a few inches tall. They have white, red, pink, and even yellow flowers. You can also ask for *R.chinensis minima*.

Other Popular Tiny Plants

Here are some other plans for your miniature garden. You may like to ask your nursery man for these particular popular plant varieties for miniature gardens – *Sedums, Muscoides, Sempervivums and Kabschia–* these are saxifrages, – dwarf varieties of irises and also *Tolmiea menziesii*. This last plant has rough leaves.

Tolmiea menziesii

Mentha requienii has a mint like fragrance. It also has blue flowers. It is one of the smallest of flowering plants.

Armeria caespitosa – also known as the small thrift – is a charming plant. You can also try grasses especially blue eye grass – *Sisyrinchium Bermudiana* and *S. californicum*. These have blue and yellow flowers. The leaves are small and rush like.

Taking Care of Your Miniature Garden

Once you have planted your miniature garden never let it dry out. It needs daily attention. You may want to place it outside occasionally during a warm shower. This washes the foliage, and gives it a breath of fresh air.

On the other hand, make sure that standing in the rain has not waterlogged your garden.

Miniature gardens, which are made in large dishes are probably too unwieldy to drain except through drainage holes. But gardens in smaller containers can be turned gently onto their sides to let the surplus water or moisture drain out.

Bulbs for Your Garden

Bulbs which are grown indoors can give you lots of pleasure since their development can be watched from start to finish. Their blooms appear at times when flowers in your garden outside are scarce. Bulbs are showy and beautiful and often delightfully fragrant.

Selecting the Right Bulbs

Selecting the right bulbs is done by using heavy and solid bulbs from your nursery. They should be free from mildew and blemish. Make sure that the tips are undamaged and that the thin outer skins, or the "tunics" are reasonably intact. This care has to be taken when you are choosing tulips.

Those bulbs, which look skinned may have been handled roughly. Such bulbs may probably do well in a garden, but they are not going to grow so well indoors.

Choose bulbs that have been specially treated to flower at certain times of the year. Depending on your locality, experienced gardeners can tell you all about the sprouting time.

A bulb normally requires a long period at low temperature, after it has been planted, followed by warmth as it reaches the flowering time. By artificially simulating these natural conditions, through subjecting your bulbs to cold or heat treatment, a number of growers are able to vary the length of waiting periods.

In this way, an experienced grower can dictate the time of the year at which a bulb is going to bloom.

Hyacinth, Iris, tulip and crocus are excellent bulb choices

This enables them to shift bulbs to any part of the world. It also enables the indoor gardener to buy with confidence, bulbs that have been specially prepared to flower early. Or perhaps at specific times during spring or in the early summer.

Planting Your Bulbs

Bulbs can be planted in many different kinds of containers held with a number of growing medias.

In beginner is probably going to use flowerpots filled with soil. To guard against overwatering, put a few pieces of broken pots covered with leaves over drainage holes. You can also get specially made bowls for bulb growing at nurseries. These are filled with special bulb fiber and medium grade peat.

One or two lumps of charcoal at the bottom of each bowl are going to give you sufficient drainage.

Planting Hyacinth and Crocus Corms

Hyacinths are planted close together, but they should not touch. The soil is packed so that the necks of your Hyacinth bulbs show over the surface.

Plant the crocus corms so that they are just covered by the soil. Level off the soil at least half an inch below the rim of your bowl.

For crocus, you can ask for special pots made of terra-cotta. These have holes punched out at intervals around the sides. Figure the parts gradually with fiber and poke a tip of the crocus corm through each hole from the inside as you continue filling. Plant several more on the top.

Early flowering crocuses in the spring are a thing of beauty and a joy forever

Each crocus pot is going to hold about a dozen corms and makes a delightful picture when all of them come to flower with blossoms along the side of the pot as well as on the top.

Most of the bulbs can be grown in soil, bulb fiber, compost, brick rubble, water, peat, and even believe it or not in bowls of wet newsprint. They just need something to hold them together, including coconut fiber.

The chief essential is to maintain an even amount of moisture. The planting material must never become waterlogged. It should never dry out. Food is often less consequence because a bulb usually stores enough of food within itself to bring it to flower.

If you are using soil, look for the best potting compost. You can also make up a mixture of sifted loam, coarse sand and peat in equal parts. This soil must be firm in your pot, but it should not be hard packed.

Bulb Fiber – Tips

Bulb fiber can be mixed at home from Peat-sedge peat, if you can find it, – a little crushed charcoal, and even oyster shell. However, a number of nursery men are going to provide you with ready mixed fiber at reasonable prices. In some cases they may also give you a fiber mix with a little bit of fertilizer.

Soak the fiber before use, but never let it swim in water. So the fiber when squeezed, is going to expose just a little bit of moisture. When it does so, it is ready for planting. Half fill the container with fiber. Stand the bulbs in place close to each other, but they should not be actually touching.

Using the handle of a wooden spoon, pack more fiber around the bulbs and until the smaller ones are completely covered and only the necks of hyacinths and Narcissus are showing a bit above the surface.

Do not twist any of these bulbs round and round to set them lower in the bowl. This is going to consolidate the fiber beneath them, so that the roots cannot penetrate the soil. They therefore grow upward and over the rim of the container. This fiber like soil should be pressed firmly into the container, but should not be packed hard.

Newspaper Compost

You can recycle them, or you can also use them for compost.

Try this experiment. Make compost from old newspapers. Newspapers are normally made up of cellulose and they have a natural tendency toward moisture. So you can prepare a newspaper composed by soaking the papers well, then shredding them into pieces the size of a pea. This soaking and shredding is also one of the beginning stages of papier-mâché. This composes now going to be used in bowls in the same way as you use fiber.

"Plunging" Bulbs

Once you have planted your bulbs put them in a cold dark place for 8 to 10 weeks to encourage good root formation. Without this plunging process bulb growing cannot be successful.

Most bulb failures are caused by bringing the bowls too early into the light and warmth.

Ideally, your bulbs are going to be plunged under a 6 inch layer of wood ashes, sand or soil in the garden. But wrap them first in polythene to save them from getting scratched and to prevent heavy rain from flooding them.

If you do not have any garden land in which to plunge them, the bowls should be stood in a cold fire less area such as a cool cupboard or in a cellar. First wrap these bowls in black polythene. This is going to keep the light out and prevent them from drying out.

Bowls wrapped in polythene will not need watering throughout the plunge.

If they are not wrapped, they should be looked at, occasionally, and supplied with sufficient water to keep the fiber just moist.

Examine the bulbs occasionally. When the bulb shoots are about 1 inch high, the root growth is sufficient strong. The container can now be brought in from the garden or taken from the cupboard.

Remove the polythene wrapping and then put them in a light cool room at a temperature about 10°C.

For the first day keep the bulbs covered with newspaper to allow the white shoots to accustom themselves to the light. They gradually done during and begin to grow vigorously, but do not take them into real warmth, which is higher than 60°F or 16°C until the leaves are well out of the bulbs.

At this stage you need to water them more frequently. That is going to depend on the heat of the room.

Keep the fiber moist to the touch, but no wetter. If it is over watered it is going to harden on top and dry out underneath. This hard top is going to repel any further moisture.

A good idea is to sprinkle the container with grass seed –agrostis tenuis. By the time your bulbs are ready to flower, you are going to have a nice green carpet of grass covering the surface of the fiber and the soil.

Growing Bulbs on Water

Crocus, Narcissus and other Narcissus varieties can be grown entirely on water. These bulbs must be kept just clear of the water. If they touch it they will start to rot. Just make sure that the roots can go down for moisture. It is not necessary to keep water grown bulbs for a time in darkness. Their development can therefore be watched daily.

Methods of Water Cultivation

This is normally done in bulb glasses, which you can buy in your nursery in different sizes. A bulb glass has a restricted neck in which the bulb is going to porch, sending its roots down to the water below. Always keep a lump of charcoal in the glass.

Rainwater is excellent for growing bulbs. I normally put out a container out in the rain, and by morning, I have fresh rain collected in that utensil.

Do not do this in the first shower of the rainy season. This first shower is going to wash all the chemical pollutants in the air, and send them deep into the soil. This chemically polluted rainy water is definitely not good for your plants. By the time you have the third shower of the season, you are going to be getting your pure Rainwater.

You can also try piling up pebbles in a bowl with water at the bottom. The bulbs are lodged between the pebbles so that they do not touch the water.

Bulb Failure

1. Stunted growth due to insufficient time in the cupboard or in the plunge bed.

2. Leaving your containers in a draught. This is going to turn the leaves yellow

3. Insufficient water at the root. This is going to cause stunted flowers, stems, dead foliage, and also did.

4. Insufficient light. This is going to cause yellowing long and lanky leaves.

Best Bulbs Choices

Hyacinths – found in pink, red, white, blue and yellow shades. Roman hyacinths are dainty and smaller. Plant these hyacinths in September or October, or according to advice from your nearest horticulturist.

Muscari – these bulbs like the cold.

Narcissus and **daffodils** – try the white, lemon, clear yellow and orange varieties. If you are growing them on pebbles, try *Paper White* and *Cragford*.

Crocuses and **tulips** can be chosen from catalogs, especially those ones which single early. Try potting them in the early autumn, so that they can flower in late winter.

Tulips come in a variety of colors and shades

Conclusion

I hope this book gives you lots of information on a brand-new look at the miniature gardening, indoor gardening, and growing bulbs for beginners. This is extremely satisfying, especially when you are trying a brand-new hobby to relax you. Best of all, you have the visible results of your efforts right in front of you.

Gardening does not need wide-open spaces, when you have sun and air and a container, a fork and a spoon, a bottle, some plants, some soil and some enthusiasm around.

So the next time you want to try your hand out at something new, which is going to keep you busy, give you hours of unalloyed pleasure, try miniature gardening or indoor gardening or even bottle gardening!

Live long and prosper.

Author Bio

Dueep Jyot Singh is a Management and IT Professional who managed to gather Postgraduate qualifications in Management and English and Degrees in Science, French and Education while pursuing different enjoyable career options like being an hospital administrator, IT,SEO and HRD Database Manager/ trainer, movie scriptwriter, theatre artiste and public speaker, lecturer in French, Marketing and Advertising, ex-Editor of Hearts On Fire (now known as Solstice) Books Missouri USA, advice columnist and cartoonist, publisher and Aviation School trainer, ex- moderator on Medico.in, banker, student councilor ,travelogue writer ... among other things! One fine morning, she decided that she had enough of killing herself by Degrees and went back to her first love -- writing. It's more enjoyable! She already has 48 published academic and 14 fiction- in- different- genre books under her belt.

When she is not designing websites or making Graphic design illustrations for clients , she is browsing through old bookshops hunting for treasures, of which she has an enviable collection – including R.L. Stevenson, O.Henry, Dornford Yates, Maurice Walsh, C.N.Williamson, Sapper, Bartimeus and the crown of her collection- Dickens "The Old Curiosity Shop," and so on... Just call her "Renaissance Woman") - collecting herbal remedies, acting like Universal Helping Hand/Agony Aunt, or escaping to her dear mountains for a bit of exploring, collecting herbs and plants and trekking.

Check out some of the other JD-Biz Publishing books

[Gardening Series on Amazon](https://amazon.com)

Health Learning Series

GRANDMA'S
NATURAL REMEDIES AND ANCIENT HERBAL BEAUTY RECIPES
Volume 1
HEALTH LEARNING SERIES
DUEEP J SINGH AND J DAVIDSON
GRANDMA'S
NATURAL REMEDIES AND ANCIENT HERBAL BEAUTY RECIPES
Volume 2
HEALTH LEARNING SERIES
DUEEP J SINGH AND J DAVIDSON
GRANDMA'S
NATURAL REMEDIES AND ANCIENT RECIPES
GRANDMA'S CURE FOR OBESITY
GRANDMA'S CURE FOR THE COMMON COLD
Volume 3
HEALTH LEARNING SERIES
DUEEP J SINGH AND J DAVIDSON
GRANDMA'S
NATURAL REMEDIES AND ANCIENT HERBAL RECIPES
Volume 4
HEALTH LEARNING SERIES
DUEEP J SINGH AND J DAVIDSON
GRANDMA'S
HERBAL LORE
ANCIENT HERBAL RECIPES AND REMEDIES
Volume 5
HEALTH LEARNING SERIES
DUEEP J SINGH AND J DAVIDSON
GRANDMA'S
ANCIENT BEAUTY REMEDIES FROM HER KITCHEN
Volume 6
HEALTH LEARNING SERIES
DUEEP J SINGH AND J DAVIDSON
GRANDMA'S
EASY TO USE TIPS IN THE KITCHEN AND OUTDOORS
Volume 7
HEALTH LEARNING SERIES
DUEEP J SINGH AND J DAVIDSON
GRANDMA'S
HOUSEHOLD HINTS AND RECIPES USING TIME TESTED ECONOMICAL TIPS IN YOUR HOME
75 Tips
Remove Stains
Peel Tomatoes
Perfect Pies
HEALTH LEARNING SERIES
DUEEP J SINGH AND J DAVIDSON
GRANDMA'S
NATURAL REMEDIES AND ANCIENT RECIPES
ALL 5 BOOKS IN 1
HEALTH LEARNING SERIES
DUEEP J SINGH AND J DAVIDSON

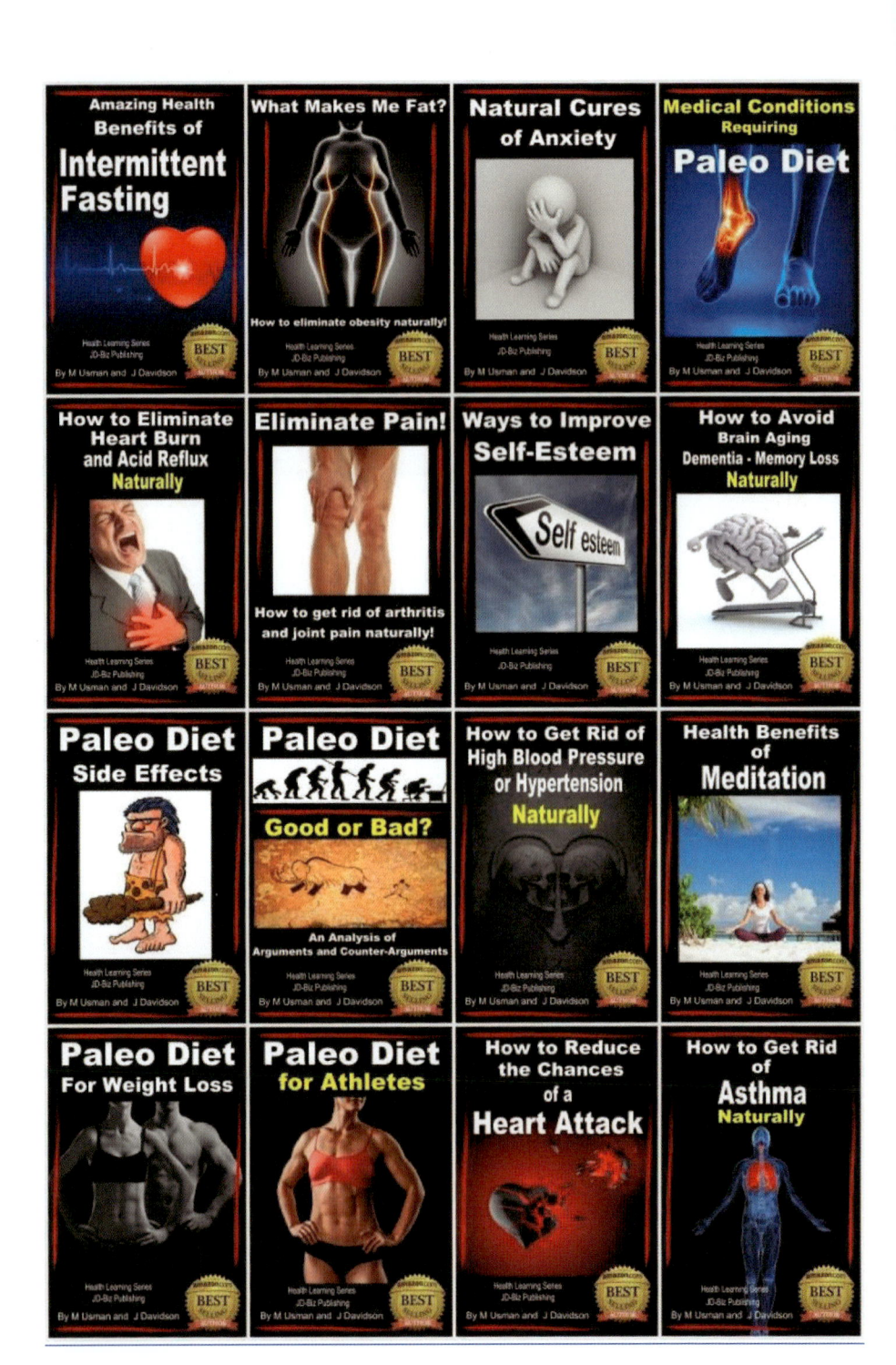

The Beginner's Guide to Indoor and Miniature Gardens   Page 60

Amazing Animal Book Series

The Beginner's Guide to Indoor and Miniature Gardens

Learn To Draw Series

The Beginner's Guide to Indoor and Miniature Gardens — Page 62

How to Build and Plan Books

The Beginner's Guide to Indoor and Miniature Gardens

Entrepreneur Book Series

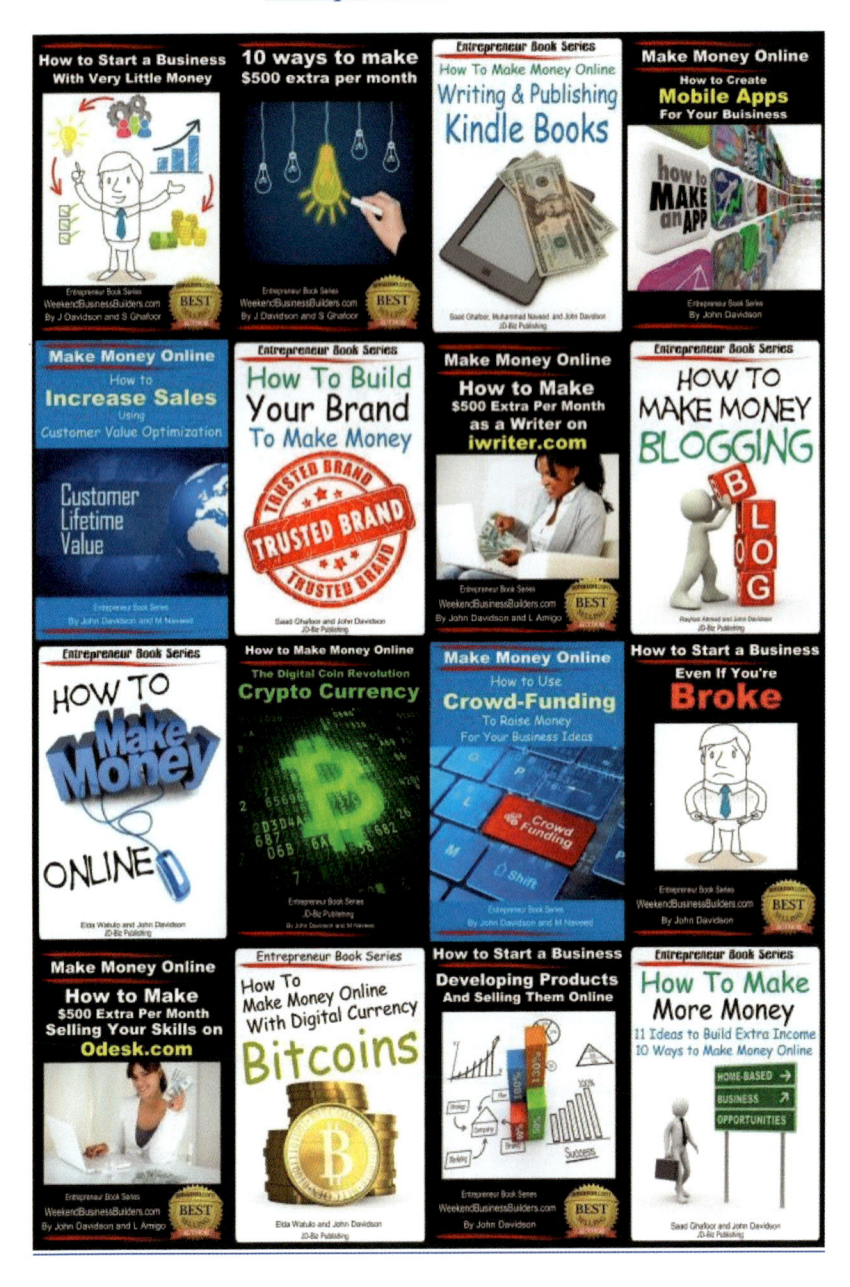

Our books are available at

1. Amazon.com
2. Barnes and Noble
3. Itunes
4. Kobo
5. Smashwords
6. Google Play Books

Download Free Books!

http://MendonCottageBooks.com

Publisher

JD-Biz Corp

P O Box 374

Mendon, Utah 84325

http://www.jd-biz.com/

Printed in Great Britain
by Amazon